# Seeing Things

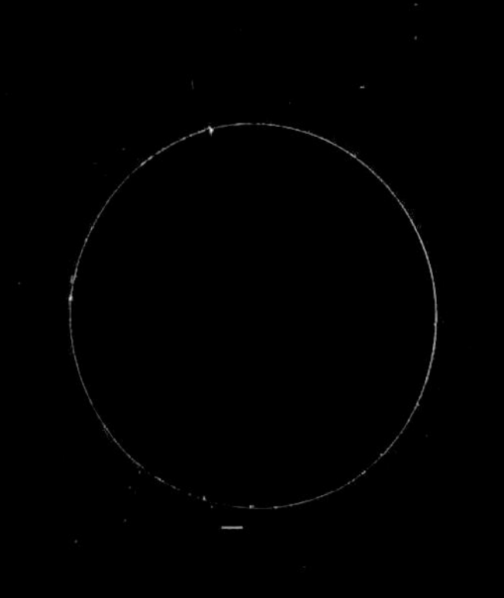

# Seeing Things

A Kid's Guide
to Looking at Photographs

by Joel Meyerowitz

aperture

# Seeing the World Around You

**I chose the photographs in this book with the hope that the things you discover in them will encourage you to open your eyes and your mind so that you can see the world around you in a new way.**

These photographs, of people and animals, of landscapes and life on the street, are full of humor, mystery, and surprise and show that any moment of any ordinary day has the potential to activate your mind with a sudden flash of insight.

That moment of **seeing** is like

**waking up.**

How lucky we are to be living in an age when making a photograph is available to everyone with a smartphone or a camera. The photographs that follow show the kinds of tools that photographers use, like intuition, timing, point of view, a willingness to wait, and the courage to move closer—tactics that make beauty and meaning, otherwise hidden, visible. All of these things are part of how you naturally see, but you have to be aware of them if you're *really going to see*.

**What you notice will reflect the way the world speaks to you, and only to you.**

You may or may not be able to change the world, but the world can certainly change you.

—Joel Meyerowitz

# Timing Is Everything

Timing *is* everything. We say that so often, when an athlete takes a perfect swing at a ball or dives to make a great catch, or when a comedian delivers the joke's punch line and everyone laughs.

But for photographers like Henri Cartier-Bresson timing is about saving a disappearing moment from the flow, and oblivion, of passing time—about finding what he called the "decisive moment."

Cartier-Bresson was walking behind the Gare Saint-Lazare train station in Paris when he saw this makeshift walkway over a puddle and a man making a running and, as we can see, futile jump in the air to avoid getting wet.

**Cartier-Bresson, with his camera always at the ready, made this fantastic "catch" of the man in mid-air—**

his heel hovers just above the water, as does the heel of his shadowy reflection. The picture doesn't show the splash, but the instant just before when the man and his mirror image are about to touch the water. Now that's timing! The splash might have made a funnier picture, but this one captures the suspense of what's about to happen.

But looking more closely, there is more to be seen here than the action of the leaping man. On the back wall there is a poster for a ballet company, and in it the dancer is leaping just like the man. Cartier-Bresson saw that too and knew that this mirroring would be seen by anyone who looked carefully at the photograph.

**Timing is about seeing what is happening, what is *about to happen*, and *where* it is taking place,**

which isn't easy to do.

Near the poster, on the far side of the fence, a man is looking in just as Cartier-Bresson is. Except Cartier-Bresson had a camera and made the photograph.

Henri Cartier-Bresson, *Behind the Gare Saint-Lazare*, 1932

# The Past in the Present

This photograph was made in Paris over a hundred years ago by Eugène Atget, who took pictures all over the city as it was changing and becoming more modern. He wanted to make a record of the people and places of that time before they disappeared and were forgotten. People looked and dressed differently then, but when I was kid a few street musicians still played street organs, portable music boxes like this one.

## The man in the picture is an organ-grinder; the young girl is most likely his daughter—

they were entertainers, making music and singing for pennies on the streets.

I am sure Atget asked them to sing for him while he made this photograph—he had to set up a large wooden camera on a tripod. He watched the old man grind out the same tune once again, but in this moment the man lifted his head just slightly—maybe he felt a sense of pride because Atget wanted to take his picture. At that same instant, the girl rested her outstretched hand on the organ and drew its vibrations into herself as she sent her song to the heavens.

Look carefully at her face.
She seems carried away by joy, or so her smile suggests. Only someone like

## Atget,

who understood the theater of the streets and the precise timing of gestures, could have

## anticipated this current of pure emotion and captured it in a picture.

Street musicians perform in big cities now, but they look like us and play instruments we're more familiar with. Photography makes it possible to time travel, to visit the past; it can extend a single moment from one time into another. One day, this time too will look distant and strange.

Eugène Atget, *Organ-grinder*, 1898–99

# Actions and Angles

## There is a wonderful geometry to this photograph.

The girl in the middle tosses a pot of water, perhaps at some kids we can't see but imagine might be there, just outside the frame. Eugene Richards catches the swish of the water mid-air as it forms an almost complete circle. Just below the girl, a woman sits in a kiddie pool (another circle) while a triangle of water sprays from the fire hydrant.

## The whole picture is tilted—the bridge, the fence, and the building come together in a zigzag of diagonal lines—and yet it's beautiful because of that.

When you look at this picture (or any picture), you realize it doesn't just exist; someone made it.

You can tell this picture was made spontaneously, which gives it its energy. In a more controlled moment, the photographer might have been tempted to straighten the frame. I suspect that Richards was a passenger in a car—his point of view seems to be from a lower angle than if he was just walking by. Of course, it could be that he was out on the street, and when he saw the girl about to throw the water, he lifted his camera in time to catch her swing.

But none of that matters in the end because Richards saw all the actions and angles of the place and had a sense of how to get everything in the frame and make it fit just right.

Eugene Richards, *Grandmother, Brooklyn, 1993*

Bruce Davidson, *New York City, Subway*, 1980

# In the In-Between Places

How much of your time is spent *in between* places, going from class to class, taking the bus, walking over to a friend's house? It's easy to think of that time as blank, as a space before or after things happen.

Bruce Davidson has spent a lot of time photographing in the subways of New York City. One afternoon he was on an elevated platform waiting for a train when he saw two women—they look a bit like glamorous models in an ad, the way the breeze blows their dresses in lovely lines around their legs. Then he noticed the street below and the way it angles into the rails and the platform, both sides of which race away into the distance. Finally, he saw the sun-struck red-brick building and included it in the frame, which adds color at the edge and in a small way connects us to the girl in the red dress.

**It would be easy to say, "Not much is happening here," but the picture holds our attention.**

The wind fills this photograph, as Davidson brings the hard edges of the city together with the softness of the forms. The sunlight of late afternoon slides across the platform and sets the scene with beautiful color.

Life is going on everywhere, all the time, and is full of small incidents—the slant of the light, its color, or the way a breeze catches someone's clothes. By noticing these kinds of details and how they play with and against each other, you can build a silent film in your mind that becomes more interesting as you add more details to what you see.

For the few minutes Davidson stood on the platform, he was wide-awake to the possibilities in this in-between place, its secret theater. There's no story here, no event of any significance, but the colors, the shapes, the people, and the wind, all make something out of nothing.

# The Power of Observation

Very few photographers make us laugh about a dog's life, or a human's, as often as Elliott Erwitt. He has a special way of seeing animals and their owners that always has a crazy twist.

I imagine him walking home and passing this person sitting on the stoop with his, or is it her?, bulldogs: one is grumpy-looking and sits off on its own; the other is serenely perched on its owner's lap.

## Erwitt instantly saw the possibilities of the scene,

and by placing himself dead center on the lapdog, he invented this hilarious bulldog-human hybrid. If he'd been standing even slightly to the left or right, this totem-like creature wouldn't exist, and the picture wouldn't be funny.

The world is full of surprising combinations so when you recognize one and unlock its potential for humor, or for whatever it is that strikes you, make a note of it so you can hold onto your observation. You could capture this insight in a photograph or in a piece of writing, but it's important to record things when and as you see them—that's how art is made, and how a larger vision of your own is formed.

## The things that *you* notice reveal how you see the world.

No two people in the same place at the same time ever see the same thing.

Elliott Erwitt, *New York City*, 2000

Garry Winogrand, *New York World's Fair, 1964*

# The Frieze

When I look at this photograph of eight people sitting on a park bench, I see tenderness in a comforting touch and a shared secret, explaining and listening, watching and reading, and

**the grace of ordinary gestures.**

The early Greeks built their temples to incorporate friezes, decorative horizontal bands above the columns. In them, a line of sculpted figures often recline, crouch, sit, stand, run, ride on horseback, carry water, play musical instruments, fight, love, and fill the space with almost every other kind of human activity that defined life two thousand years ago. But Winogrand saw more than just what was happening with the frieze of figures on the bench. His gaze continued on to the much smaller frieze of figures in the distance.

This kind of seeing, of noticing subjects both near and far at the same time, is something photography does very well.

In this picture,

**the repetition between the foreground and background is musical; the top of the frame supports the melody of the figures on the bench.**

I don't think Winogrand was thinking about Greek buildings, friezes, or music when he made this photograph of people lined up on a bench, but he clearly saw the beauty in the rhythm of their gestures, in the way their bodies turn toward and twist away from each other, the drama between the three girls in the middle, and the richness of all the possible meanings we can take from them.

# Hidden Texts

Melanie Einzig loves being on the street in the middle of things. She has an eye for unexpected coincidences and the quick wit to recognize a lot of small stories happening all at once.

At first, there might not have been too much happening on this street corner, but then someone walked into the frame, and then another person came along, and then another. She paid attention as people started to walk through the space in front of her and noticed how they formed temporary connections with each other and created new stories.

I can imagine Einzig **talking to herself (as she *reads* the hidden text of the street):**

"What a nice, sunny day; oh, look at that couple hugging. . . . Uh, oh, this guy with the baseball cap is staggering and looks like he's going to fall. I better keep an eye on him in case he needs help. . . . Wow, here comes a guy with a white parrot on his shoulder. . . . Wait, where'd that dog come from?" I have always believed that "if you can say it, you can see it." If you can *read* these brief events happening in front of you that otherwise would have nothing to do with each other, you can begin to *see* them.

Try standing on a corner, or anywhere that you like to hang out, and just watch what strange juxtapositions the world brings to you. With this kind of observation, you read a situation as it unfolds. You can list the things you see silently to yourself (almost like a game of I-Spy)—if you say it, you can see it.

These stories, these relationships, begin and end in a moment, and they only happen because of the camera, because of the frame.

**Because you stopped to look,**

and read.

Melanie Einzig, *Spring Corner, New York*, 2000

Sally Gall, *Flying*, 2014

# Light and Happiness

If a friend asked you, “Did you do anything interesting today,” and you answered, “I looked at some laundry,” she would probably think you were nuts. Laundry? What about it? A lot of things that might inspire you don’t sound so interesting, but you can see something that charges you, astonishes you, in a split second.

People ask me all the time, **“How do I know what to take a picture of?”**

And I answer, **“Whatever it is that makes you stop, photograph that!”**

With this photograph, Sally Gall shows us how surprising, and sculptural, laundry can be. As Gall passed under laundry lines hanging between buildings in Siracusa, Italy, she glanced up and saw sun-struck colors floating and billowing above her, like sails filling with wind.

She must have been stunned by the way

**these common objects— sheets, tablecloths, and towels— were transformed by light and air.**

I can imagine her standing there transfixed by the playful movement overhead, and then inspired to take her camera out. Although the photograph is *of* laundry, it isn’t *about* laundry. This is a photograph about wind. Or color. Or light. Or happiness. Or is it about all of those things?

# Man and Beast

## Just look at that incredible ear and horn!

And the gerenuk seems to be standing on one leg, like a mythical creature from an ancient cave painting. Gerenuks are *wild* animals, yet look how at ease the sheikh is as the gerenuk's hoof rests on his shoulder, and how much affection there seems to be between them.

## Richard Avedon's photograph of these two different beings—nearly the same height—shows the trust and bond that exists between them.

## The stark light creates a bright glow behind them,

almost like a white-paper background would in a photo studio. Avedon used the sunlight to silhouette the figures, and in doing so, the man and gerenuk cast their shadows toward the foreground, becoming part of our world rather than an imaginary one, which makes their friendship even more powerful.

When you look carefully at the way people relate to animals, there are many curious and revealing things to see. These two are completely different, but the *connection* between them is wholly familiar, universal.

Richard Avedon, *Sheikh Saud Al-Thani of Qatar with Gerenuk, St. Louis Zoo, Missouri, January 11, 2000*

# The Right Moment

## The elephant is so magnificent that you might think that's what this photograph is about.

When I first saw the picture, I was excited by the physical presence of the elephant and the way his heavy trunk looped around his trainer's neck.

The elephant is great to look at with his massive head and legs, large floppy ear, furry hairdo, and all those folds and wrinkles. And the trainer stands there at ease, the weight of the trunk seemingly as light and comfortable as a scarf around his neck.

## Mary Ellen Mark was quick to notice the little details that give the picture its grace:

the belt and the trainer's hands, the bracelets so perfectly positioned that they follow the curve of the belt, which echoes the loop of the trunk, and then the intense look of the trainer's face.

The picture needed to go beyond its spectacular subject and perfect geometry. Once Mark got the pieces in place, she knew to wait. I'm sure she took a lot of pictures of the elephant and trainer in this pose.

Mary Ellen Mark, *Ram Prakash Singh with His Elephant Shyama, Great Golden Circus, Ahmedabad, India*, 1990

But when she saw that both man and beast were giving her the dead-eye stare, as if they'd both had enough, she immediately knew that the right moment was *now*!

# Eye Contact

The faces we encounter every day are full of movement. Smiles and expressions flicker for a moment and disappear; eyes widen, sparkle, blink, and close.

Heads nod, tilt, and turn. This constant animation changes our impression of a person second by second. We add the sequence together to form a momentary understanding of who the person is. Rarely do we have a chance to look at a face with the stillness that a photograph allows.

## Feel the intensity of the boy's stare.

This photograph invites us to make direct eye contact, to look for a long time into the face of another human being, and to inspect the details. The picture allows you to have a connection with the person in this portrait even though he is from a different time. It's hard to look away.

We can't know what the boy's expression means, but Paul Strand recognized something vital in it, and that's why he made this photograph. They may have just met, but Strand was able to get close, to get the boy to settle down before the camera and reveal something of himself.

## While he is looking at Strand, he also seems to be looking inward, contemplating his own thoughts.

This portrait preserves a moment, but it is the connection between the photographer and subject *in the moment* that makes this portrait one that others want to look at again and again. This particular magic happened in 1951, but it happens again every time someone looks into this boy's eyes.

Paul Strand, *Young Boy, Gondeville, Charente, France*, 1951

# The Blue Hour

We may not have the night vision of an owl or a wolf, but there is still plenty for us to see in the dusky hours of evening. At twilight, the world is reinvented for a brief time. Details grow hazy; forms combine to make new shapes. Subtle tones of color are there to be discovered.

Jonathan Smith has a love of darkness and the way it transforms the things we see. The picture is incredibly simple: the massive forms of the bridge foundation, a few lines of lace work in the tower, and then the nearby buildings. The sky and snow-covered street are nearly the same luminous blue, and the two electric lights are the only other accents.

**But Smith saw the mood of the place, the way it felt like a film set or a dream.**

He constructed this picture out of very little material in a fading moment. Yet, when I look at it, I long to be there, to stand in that hour, in that place, and feel the bridge leaping across the river and disappearing into the shroud of mist.

**This photograph is a poem.**

Jonathan Smith, *Manhattan Bridge, Twilight*, 2008

# Still Life

## Every day we pick things up and put them down, immediately forgetting them. William Eggleston finds them for us.

He looks at the world with a collector's eye, charmed and astonished by objects that he finds visually interesting—all of which he gathers with his camera. This ordinary bottle, glowing like a ruby, caught Eggleston's eye, and he made *it* the subject of his picture.

**As familiar as a bottle of soda is, here it is presented as a luminous, floating, double-image of itself—the bottle stands on its own elongated reflection.**

It is as strange as it is ordinary. The red taillights of the other car (which are also glowing but not as brightly) link the bottle and the glints of sunlight together. The shadows of the surrounding trees (which we don't see in the picture) frame the scene and add to this quiet pause in the afternoon.

The fact that Eggleston stopped to photograph this surprising moment of beauty reminds us to look more carefully, to remember that the most banal objects, the most commonplace afternoons, contain unexpected mystery and wonder.

William Eggleston, *Untitled (Los Alamos portfolio)*, 1965–74

# Seeing the Light

All of us have seen light shining into dark spaces: a movie theater when the projector shoots its arrow of light at the screen or sunbeams breaking through the mist on a foggy morning.

## Light is elemental and everywhere, as sunlight, moonlight, starlight, firelight, streetlight, candlelight, even as lasers and neon.

To "see the light" is to understand something more clearly or in a new way, as in Abelardo Morell's photograph of light beams falling in a polka-dotted pattern on the floor.

## The light cuts through the darkness, drawing our attention and changing the familiar into the enchanted.

## The rays travel through the air in pencil lines and end as circles.

The way light looks can be the whole reason for taking a picture. It's fun to chase sunbeams. Where is the light and what is it becoming?

Abelardo Morell, *Light Entering Our House*, 2004

# Shadow Play

Your shadow, like a faithful dog, is always at your side—a companion that demands nothing of you and, in return, requires no attention.

## Your shadow seems to just tag along. But you animate it; you are its director.

While it moves with you and does whatever you do, your shadow is also a kind of elastic distortion of you. It stretches out when the sun is low; it crawls up walls. Your shadow can go places you can't.

Lee Friedlander has made his shadow perform all kinds of stunts over the years. His shadow-actor makes jokes, meets new friends, watches TV, wears outrageous hats, and plays in the dirt. Here, he becomes a fantastic scarecrow with crazy hair, rocky body parts, and lopsided legs. Is he standing up or is he lying down?

Of course the actor and the director are the same person.

## Friedlander is always on the lookout for new ways to see what trouble his shadow can get into, and how much fun he can have watching it.

Lee Friedlander, *Canyon de Chelly, Arizona*, 1983

# Making Fun

People love to visit monuments: the Statue of Liberty, the Eiffel Tower, the Leaning Tower of Pisa. Where there's a monument, there are tourists making pictures of their family and friends in front of it. The Leaning Tower of Pisa provokes some the craziest behaviors of all and may be the most fun to watch.

**Martin Parr clearly has a good sense of humor.**

He watched all the wacky stuff taking place on the field in front of the tower as people played the game of holding it up, or catching it as it fell, and then found the whimsy in people doing this at the same time.

**In his picture, they all seem to be taking part in a tai chi class or warming up for a spontaneous dance performance.**

Everyone tries to take the same funny or perfect postcard picture, but there's another way of finding a photograph that *only you* can see. After all, you can buy a postcard in the gift shop.

Martin Parr, *The Leaning Tower of Pisa*, 1990

# Everything All at Once

Saul Leiter liked the noisy, visual confusion of a New York City street. He liked signs piled one on top of another, reflections in windows and water. He liked when dark interrupted light. In his pictures, people dissolve in droplets or are bisected by poles and door edges—anything he can put in their way.

## This picture is a collage of bits and pieces of signs and awnings, light and shadow, red and black, people and trucks—the patterns and colors come together in a beautiful crash.

To see these kind of fragments and edges is to see graphically. It's not about the man smoking a cigarette. When you read the words—*house*, *bar*, *gin*, *warning*, *babaco*—they don't add up to a story. This picture is about how things, people, shapes, and colors come together in a kind of mash-up. Everything is happening all at once.

## So many things overlap in this picture, just as so many things overlap in life.

How many things do you have going at the same time? You listen to music, watch a video, do homework, play a game, send a text. Our computer and phone lives collide in much the same way street life did for Saul Leiter. But with his photographs, he put a frame around the messiness of life, and in that way, gave it a sense of order. Just like him, try to take it in all at once.

Saul Leiter, *Harlem*, 1960

# Watching and Waiting

**People do the strangest things. Why did this little boy force his way into the telephone booth? It looks so uncomfortable.**

These kinds of unexpected, and funny, incidents take place all the time. Sometimes you get a feeling that something exciting or surprising is about to happen—you may even be able to predict exactly what's coming—but a lot of the time you just have to watch and wait.

**Street photographer Helen Levitt saw the large woman in the phone booth with her daughter and stopped to keep an eye on the situation.**

The scene had the makings of a good photograph: the softness of the bodies squeezed into the hard lines of the telephone booth. But it was when the boy started edging himself into the booth that Levitt made the picture. The space is so tight that his head is bent back and his arm won't fit through the door.

You have to be willing to let things play out. If something seems interesting to you, hang out for a moment to see if what you *think could happen*, actually does.

**If Levitt had gotten bored and walked away, she would have missed the best part.**

Helen Levitt, *New York City (Phone Booth)*, 1984

# New Perspectives

The way we see and understand is radically altered by our point of view. Take this photograph for instance. There are some small boys in a doorway (notice that the smallest boy is carrying the biggest package!), and they're looking up at the man standing in front of them.

**We have no idea what is happening, so the picture is a puzzle.**

Gordon Parks saw the kids in the doorway, and then made a choice to kneel down and frame the picture at the same height as the boys and from underneath the man's arm. By taking the photograph from this angle, Parks was able to capture the various expressions on the boys' faces.

**Suddenly this simple scene of boys in a doorway is charged with drama. He made a choice to change his perspective, and that changed *everything*.**

Try experimenting with your perspective. Watch life from new vantage points. Lie on the ground in a spot where you would normally stand. Or stand still in a place that you would ordinarily be moving through quickly on your way to somewhere else. You may notice and, maybe, *feel* something that would be hidden from you otherwise.

Gordon Parks, *Black Muslim Schoolchildren, Chicago*, 1963

Thomas Roma, *Untitled*, from the series Mondo Cane, 2012

# A Dog's Life

Thomas Roma typically photographs in a straightforward way, but when he made a series of pictures in a dog park in Brooklyn, he went out on a limb, so to speak, by mounting his camera on the end of a homemade selfie-stick.

**He told me he was really interested in looking at dogs from above because he noticed that their shadows created two-dimensional phantom dogs.**

In this picture, the shadow looks like the real dog, while the dog looks more like the shadow. What you can't see in this photograph is how tough it was to make.

**Roma didn't know what he was shooting—he had to angle the camera out there and make a guess at what it was capturing.**

He had to imagine where the edges of the frame were. I'm sure there were lots of missed opportunities and cut-off animals, but the surprises—those pictures that worked out, like this one—are really special.

Roma was willing to experiment and improvise, and that led him to seeing in a new way and to bringing into being photographs that no one had ever seen before.

# Beautiful Chaos

**Sometimes when we're in a crowd, we feel overwhelmed. We don't know where to look or which way to go.**

But chaos always has a powerful intensity. It calls us to look at everything all at once: near and far, up and down, left and right.

The reason this is such a good photograph is that Alex Webb walked into chaos instead of retreating from it. He saw the overflowing action as an invitation to bring as many things as possible into the frame. From farther away, the scene probably just looked like a mess of kids running around in a busy playground.

**But Webb moved closer until he could see how the curving lines of the jungle gym and the moving figures of the kids created a spiderweb of energy.**

He could see where the bright sunlight made dark shadows. At the heart of all this activity is the shadow of the kid whose legs we see in the foreground. This small detail helps draw our eye further into the action, where we find the legs of another child in mid-swing. The tilting colors and slanting walls add to the wonderful tangle that is this photograph.

Chaos is said to be the opposite of order, and order, the basis for beauty. But that doesn't mean that chaos can't be beautiful too.

Alex Webb, *Children Playing in a Playground, Havana*, 2000

Walker Evans, *Billboard Painters, Florida*, 1934

# A Parallel Universe

The world as seen in a black-and-white photograph is very different from the world as we see it, and the camera magically moves us into this parallel universe—we can only see the other world through a photograph. Every color has its equivalent gray value: a blue sky is light gray, a red apple is darker gray, while a pink rose is very pale gray. When you photograph in black and white regularly, like Walker Evans did, you learn to mentally convert colors into grays.

Evans also understood the way our three-dimensional world flattens in a photograph. Taking a photograph is a lot like looking through one eye: things in the background move to the surface, there's no depth.

At first glance,

## we don't know what is what in this picture.

Two men are painting a roadside billboard, and the light gray of the sky blends perfectly with the top of the sign, so the ladder looks like it's leaning against the sky, while the little roof and flag float up above.

## The painted scene and reality fuse.

I imagine that Evans was probably amused by the way the painted tree grows next to the real one. He recognized that the blue sky, and the green trees, and the red building on the billboard would all merge in this *other* picture, a picture that is *purposefully* confusing to our eye—but it's a wonderful kind of confusion.

# The Frame Within the Frame

Stephen Shore stopped along this roadside in the middle of nowhere when he saw this billboard superimposed on the larger, similar landscape he was driving through. It even has the same color range.

**The painted, majestic landscape of the billboard completes the more ordinary-looking landscape behind it.**

At the same time, the frame within a frame merges the real and artificial landscapes and highlights how different they are from each other. The photograph incorporates these conflicting views to create double meanings and different readings.

Someone has painted over the lettering on the billboard, so we don't know where this place is—it's become more abstract than actual, more about the idea of America than a specific location on a map.

I feel sure that the way the clouds looked as they crashed into the cloudless sky of the billboard must have been part of why Shore took this picture. He saw something deeper going on and put the two landscapes together to make a visual joke, one that is both thought-provoking and funny.

Stephen Shore, *U.S. 97, South of Klamath Falls, Oregon, July 21, 1973*

## Dreamscapes

This is a photograph about reflection.

The longer you look at this picture, the more the image reveals, and that is the nature of reflection. Richard Misrach saw the slightly unreal, or surreal, properties of this landscape: the way the dune and its reflection morph into an otherworldly object, a spaceship hovering between sky and earth.

When I look at this picture in a certain way,

**the dune doesn't feel like it's rising out of the water but is suspended in the clouds.**

If you look long enough, though, you might notice that you can see the bottom of the lake and that the ground is coming up through a cloud in the lower right-hand corner.

A few centuries ago reflecting pools became popular in public parks and gardens so people could come and reflect upon their ideas. The "virtual" world of the reflection existed inside the "real" world: in those pools, as in this photograph, if the wind stirred the water, the illusion was broken.

Reflections are everywhere. It pays to look more deeply into them and allow the line between reality and illusion to blur.

Richard Misrach, *Battleground Point #21*, 1999

# Mirror Image

## Sometimes a photograph makes me look twice,

and even then it might be hard for me to understand what I am looking at.

This is a seemingly simple picture; it's easy to see that there are thousands of penguins standing around on a rocky beach. In the distance, the penguins get smaller and smaller at just the place where a mountain slopes down. This point of convergence is what divides the picture in half and makes it seem to flip. The snow-lined ridges mirror the black-and-white pattern of the penguins.

I think it's the way the picture has been divided into a top and bottom that makes it momentarily confusing. I found myself turning the picture upside down to look at it, something I don't often do with photographs.

Sebastião Salgado has a very strong sense of graphic design. His photographs are lessons in looking at spacious places and connecting the smallest details everywhere in the frame.

## This photograph wouldn't look at all the same if it were in color.

The black and white reduces the forms to pattern. Salgado presents the markings of the penguins and the rocky folds in the bowl of the mountain as visual equals. Is that enough to make this an interesting photograph?

I leave that to you, but in either case, this image is a good reminder that the world—as it appears to our eyes—can be altered just by making a photograph of it.

Sebastião Salgado, *Chinstrap Penguins on Saunders Island in South Sandwich Islands*, 2009

## There are vantage points that change the way we look at a place.

From this spot, which is from the terrace of a king, we look down on tiny figures walking outside a palace that stretches into the distance, as do the walkways of the formal gardens. In Luigi Ghirri's photograph, scale is exaggerated in such a way that it makes it seem more like a drawing or a painting, something make-believe.

It is a soft, summer afternoon, and the slightly fuzzy and warm golden light adds to the storybook quality of the picture, making it feel even more unreal. The arches repeat and seem to go on and on as if the scene is a stage set or a diorama.

## The people are the size of ants. We know they're human beings, but they're no longer human scale.

Where we choose to stand can make a big difference in scale—it can change the relative sizes of objects and alter our sense of reality.

The French have an expression for this kind of visual illusion, *trompe l'oeil* ("fool the eye"), and they were good at creating works of art that shift the perception of space in their palaces and homes. Photographs can fool the eye too.

Luigi Ghirri, *Versailles*, 1985

# The Human Condition

When we see a series of pictures together we naturally try to connect them as a story. Some photographers experiment with storytelling, linking frames to lead our imagination in creating a narrative.

Here,

## Duane Michals uses the form like a comic book.

In the first panel, a man stands on a subway platform as a train comes to a stop. Light glows in the subway car windows and from the clock above the platform. In the next frame, the man begins to dissolve in an ellipse of light as the train starts to move. By the fourth frame, the train is gone, and the ellipse of light becomes a galaxy. Finally, the man disappears altogether, and we move farther out until we see the galaxy swirling in the infinity of space. The clock has transformed into another, more distant galaxy.

## The pictures at the beginning and the end of this series are vastly different from each other.

You can't travel much farther than from a man underground in the subway to the cosmic swirl of the galaxy and beyond.

It has been said that we are all made of stardust, and so, perhaps, Michals saw his subject returning to the dust. From this idea, he connected these two very different images into a grand narrative about the "human condition." And he did it in just six pictures.

**If you started with two photographs, a beginning and an end, what story would you tell?**

Duane Michals, *The Human Condition*, 1969

# Can You See a Story?

A young man lies on the sidewalk with his arms outstretched. It looks like he's just fallen to the pavement—and that he might have been knocked down by the man with the hammer. But that's just what it *looks like*.

It's possible the man walked up the stairs from this Paris metro station, when he suddenly felt faint and collapsed. A moment later, the construction worker carrying a hammer stepped over his body. You can't know what happened the moment before, or what's happening outside the frame. You only have this visual document to go on.

**The picture doesn't have to tell a full story.**

**It has to hold your attention, sometimes in the form of a question.**

It can be ambiguous, which is when something is described and yet you're not sure what it means (it has more than one possible interpretation). Ambiguity is an important quality in art, in particular, because it can keep you, the viewer, wondering and interested. Photography has the power to record all the details and information contained in a moment, and yet, you're not quite sure of the real story.

There are as many sides to the story as there are witnesses. And a photograph shows you everything but the meaning.

Joel Meyerowitz, *Fallen Man*, *Paris*, 1967

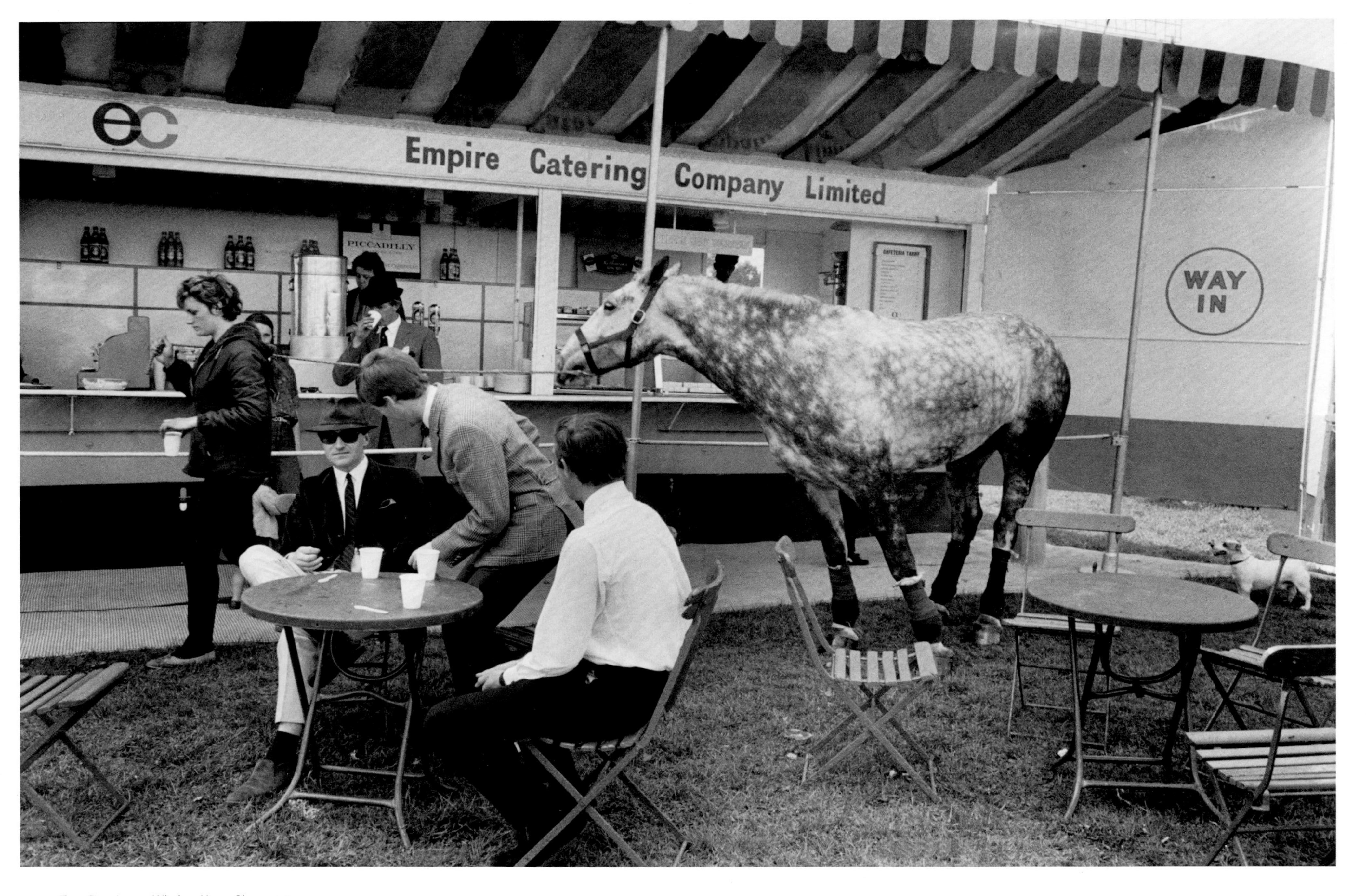


Tony Ray-Jones, *Windsor Horse Show*, 1967

# Things Aren't Always as They Seem

Tony Ray-Jones was a close friend of mine. As young photographers, we struggled to teach ourselves to look all over the space in front of us so that we could capture as many events as possible in a single photograph.

**This temporary "take away" counter at an English country fair is a great example of how ordinary scenes can be read in different, and possibly amusing, ways.**

Who is the guy in the dark shades? His sunglasses and posture make him seem like he might be a Mafia boss, but he's probably just a friend. And the young man, who looks like he's trying to please the boss, is probably just coming back from the counter with the cup of tea and taking his seat. (Notice how the horse's neck and head make a shape, almost identical to the shape of the boy's back and head—it's as if they fit together like puzzle pieces.)

**But what *is* that horse doing at the counter?**

No one else seems to notice it standing there, which is part of why this photograph is funny. I had the impression—just for a moment—that the horse was standing on a chair. These kinds of uncertain moments are part of the pleasure of seeing photographically.

# Looking Into the Future

## I have been in love with this photograph ever since I first saw it.

The girl, Lella, is traveling through the French countryside in the back of a truck. She stands out against a darkening sky as the late-summer sunlight strikes her, showing through her sheer blouse. The wind moves through her hair, which glistens slightly. Although she is young, she has a kind of easy grace and nobility that make her wonderful to look at.

## We don't know what she is looking at or where she is going.

But it doesn't matter, because this picture is about Lella looking forward into the future. The slight tilt of her body and her raised chin give us a sense of strength and determination. Édouard Boubat recognized the moment as one of transformation—a teenager becoming an adult. Her gaze becomes a symbol, a metaphor for change and the ongoing passage of time.

Every second we experience disappears as we live it. Right *now* is slipping away into the past as *you* move forward.

## But a photograph stops time and preserves fleeting beauty, such as Lella's, lifting it into something meaningful beyond the moment, into something timeless.

Édouard Boubat, *Lella, Bretagne*, 1947

I learned to see when I was a young boy in the 1940s. My father would point things out to me on the tough streets of the Bronx, and say, "Watch this," or "Pay attention," and immediately some funny interaction or event would take place. He was a real New York street-smart guy, as well as a first-rate athlete, dancer, boxer, comedian, and storyteller—all qualities that required excellent timing and made the observations he passed along to me that much sharper.

By learning to look more closely at life around me, I saw that although human activity repeats itself, the characters are different each time, so there are always new variations on the same themes. Believing this to be true made me the photographer that I am today. This is my twenty-fifth book, and I have had hundreds of exhibitions all over the world. After all this time—fifty-three years now—of making pictures, I still love the surprises that photographs introduce us to, over and over again.

No book is made all on its own. It is truly a team effort, and this book certainly had the best team I could have hoped for. Denise Wolff, the editor, has guided the writing and picture selection with a great eye, a loving hand, and a kind heart. Sarah McNear showed us the way toward making this a rich educational experience. Sonya Dyakova designed a book that I know will be a mind- and eye-catching treasure to hold. My wife, Maggie Barrett, listened to every essay countless times and helped me to pare them down to where Alexa Dilworth could come in with her fine ear for phrasing and balance to bring the essays to a final state with eloquence and grace. My studio team, led by Ember Rilleau, kept everything together and supported me brilliantly.

Many of the photographers in this book are friends and colleagues. My gratitude for their thought-provoking work is part of why this book came into being. It gave me so much pleasure to write about the great variety of ways in which we see. My thanks to Eugene, Bruce, Elliott, Melanie, Sally, Jon, Bill, Abe, Lee, Martin, Tom, Alex, Stephen, Richard, Sebastião, Duane, and, of course, to those photographers now gone, especially Garry, Mary Ellen, and Tony, who showed me the brilliance of the world.

—Joel Meyerowitz

*Seeing Things:*
***A Kid's Guide to Looking at Photographs***
**by Joel Meyerowitz**

Editor: **Denise Wolff**
Designer: **Atelier Dyakova, London**
Production Director: **Nicole Moulaison**
Production Manager: **Thomas Bollier**
Copy Editor: **Alexa Dilworth**
Senior Text Editor: **Susan Ciccotti**
Work Scholars: **David Arkin, Sophie Klafter, Cassidy Paul, and Melissa Welikson**

Additional staff of the Aperture book program includes:
**Chris Boot**, Executive Director
**Lesley A. Martin**, Creative Director
**Taia Kwinter**, Publishing Manager
**Emily Patten**, Publishing Assistant
**Elena Goukassian**, Copy Editor
**Samantha Marlow**, Associate Editor
**Lanah Swindle**, Editorial Assistant
**Brian Berding**, Designer
**Kellie McLaughlin**, Chief Sales and Marketing Officer
**Richard Gregg**, Sales Director, Books



First edition, 2016
Printed in China
10 9 8 7 6

Library of Congress Control Number: 2015953484
ISBN 978-1-59711-315-1

To order Aperture books, or inquire about gift or group orders, contact:
+1 212.946.7154
orders@aperture.org

For information about Aperture trade distribution worldwide, visit:
aperture.org/distribution

**aperture**
Aperture Foundation
548 West 28th Street, 4th Floor
New York, NY 10001
aperture.org

Aperture, a not-for-profit foundation, connects the photo community and its audiences with the most inspiring work, the sharpest ideas, and with each other—in print, in person, and online.

Image Credits

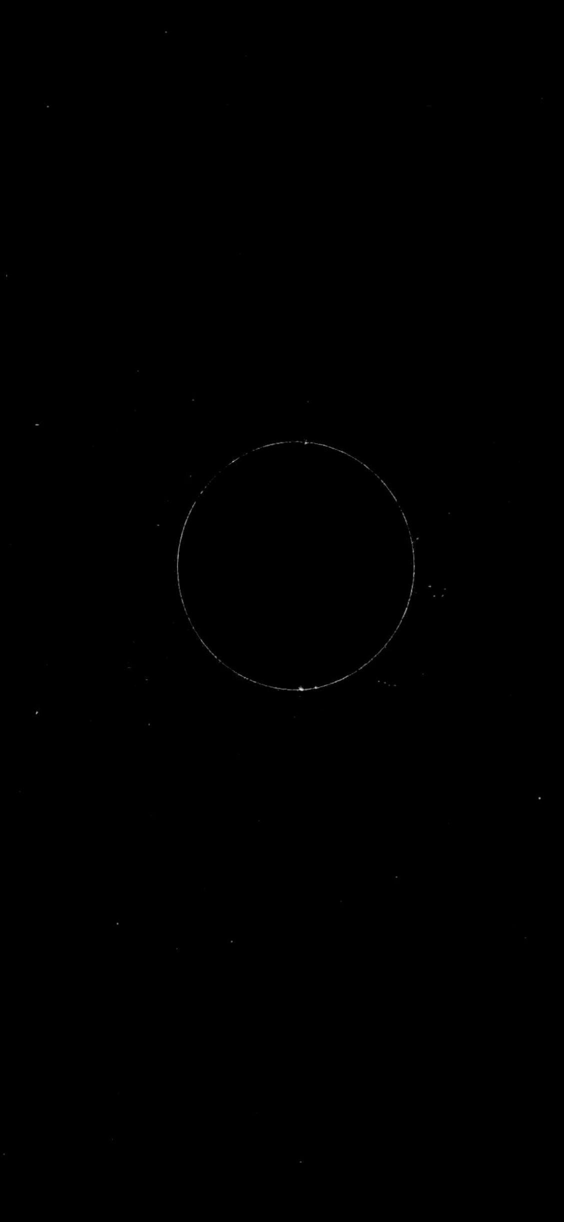

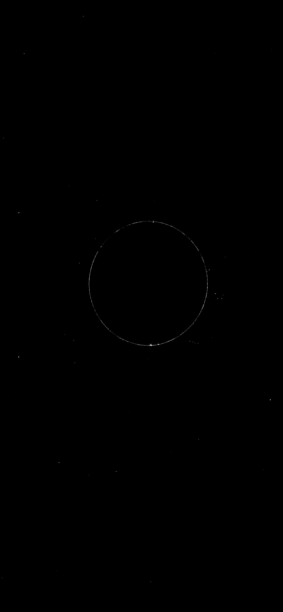

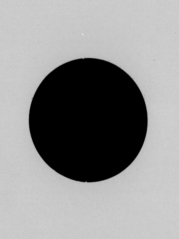